Engineering for the Uninitiated

Discover If Engineering Is Right for Your Child

Revised Edition

Yvonne Ng

illustrations by
Jack Sutter & Mary Lofgren

an Engineer's Playground book

This publication is designed to provide accurate and authoritative information on the subject matter covered. It is sold with the understanding that the author or publisher is not engaged in rendering legal, accounting, or other professional service. If legal advice or other expert assistance is required, the services of a competent professional should be sought.

This book is dedicated to the parents like Cresy and Stacy who pulled me aside and said, pointing to their children, "You need to help me be a better parent for this kid." It is also for the teachers who saw that engineering could help them be the teachers they always wanted to be for their kids.

Engineering for the Uninitiated
Revised Edition Copyright © 2018 Yvonne Ng. All rights reserved.

ISBN-13:978-1975659059
ISBN-10:1975659058

Contents

"But what do you use it for?"

—Yvonne, as a child

When I was young, my parents—both scientists—took me to their science research labs. At my father's lab, there was an electron microscope that magnified a mosquito so much I could see the details of its eyes. At my mother's lab, there was a machine that removed air from a chamber until the pressure was nearly zero. My parents proudly explained how these machines would help them uncover the secrets of nature: being able to magnify objects would unlock the secret of coal explosions, and creating a clean surface would reveal how chemicals bonded together. As scientists, they hoped to have their kid follow in their footsteps. "But what will we use that knowledge for?" I asked my poor parents. They sighed, "You probably should be an engineer."

If this question is familiar to you, your child may be an engineer in the making. This book was designed for parents who want to find out if engineering is for their kids. If you're not quite sure what engineering is, it may seem that engineers are part of a secret club with many requirements. How can you help your kid discover the fun and excitement that engineering has to offer?

This book is a gentle initiation into the world of engineering. Inside lies the results of my years of being an engineer, advising engineering students, and working with teachers and parents who are curious about the field. This is hardly a definitive or comprehensive treatise on engineering. The examples are purposefully personal and come from my own life experiences as an engineer and my interactions with other engineers. These are the stories I would share in a casual setting like a party or a picnic. I hope this, through words and pictures, serves as a useful introduction to the world of engineering so you can see if this dynamic, creative, yet pragmatic field is right for your kid.

1: What Is This Thing Called Engineering?

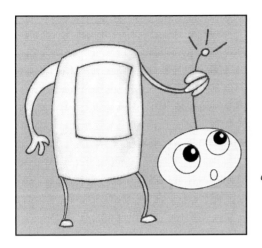

A priest, a lawyer, and an engineer were about to be executed during the French Revolution. The priest was brought up and laid down. The rope was released, but the blade of the guillotine did not fall. He declared it was divine intervention and was released. The lawyer was brought up next. He was laid down, and again, the rope was released, but the blade stayed put. He declared he could not be tried twice for the same crime and was released. The engineer was next, and as he was being laid down, he looked up at the blade and said, "Oh, I think I see your problem."

—Engineering joke

Engineers make things work. We try to get results, such as systems that we can depend on or products that move, lift, or calculate.

What are these "things"? Most people realize that "high tech" things like rockets, satellites, or airplanes are made by engineers. Often people also realize that "big" things also involve engineers: buildings, bridges, dams, power plants.

For me, though, the magic of engineering is in how the things we make affect daily life. My life, for one, would be very different without engineering: without glasses, I would be legally blind; without a prosthesis, I would not be able to walk.

In this chapter, let's look at just a few of the engineered things that surround us. Once you have developed "engineering eyes," you may never look at the world in the same way.

AT HOME

When I wake up, I am surrounded by engineered things that help me start off on the right foot—literally! I depend on engineered products and systems to make washing up efficient and comfortable.

Shampoo: Engineers create formulas that clean and condition my hair without irritating my skin. The bottle is also molded to have a pleasing shape and be unbreakable if dropped.

Light and clock: Engineers create devices that use electricity to generate light or measure time.

Glasses: Thanks to engineering, glasses can be produced in as little time as an hour. Engineers have also created new materials so my lenses are thin, light, shatterproof plastic, not thick and heavy glass.

Toilet: While engineers have made advances in toilets that conserve water during flushing, they also are responsible for the whole system that brings water in and takes waste away—and purifies it!

Prosthetic leg: The material used in my prosthesis has been made lighter and stronger by engineering. My prosthetic foot has also been engineered to have some bounce and to flex in multiple ways so that my movements feel as natural and comfortable as possible.

OUT AND ABOUT

Whether I drive, walk, or take public transit, I encounter the results of engineering.

Buildings: Engineers translate the creative vision of architects into reality, coordinate groups of workers during construction, and make sure details like heating, plumbing, lighting, and electrical outlets are installed correctly.

Road: The building of roads, where they are placed, how they are used during repairs, and planning for current and future traffic are some of the responsibilities of engineers.

Light rail: Transportation systems and the vehicles that travel on them are all possible because of engineers.

Traffic control: Engineering decisions include whether a stop sign or light is required to minimize accidents but maximize the traffic flow.

Pressurized water: Drinking fountains have been engineered for human comfort and convenience via pumpls that deliver water from wells or mainline pipes

Pedestrian bridge: When designing the overall structure, engineeers must take into account the number of people who might walk or stand on it at one time and elements such as rain, ice, or wind.

Water management: Engineers design outlets for run-off water so the ground is not oversaturated by gutter flow, sloped roads, or heavy rainfall.

LIVING WELL

Engineering has made my quality of life better. Now I can feed myself any time of day, any time of year, with mostly what I want when I want it. I can also get medical attention for conditions that have blinded or even killed people in the past.

Television: The ability to bring live action and sound to places thousands of miles apart requires mastery of electronic technology and network systems.

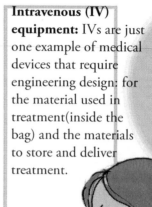

Intravenous (IV) equipment: IVs are just one example of medical devices that require engineering design: for the material used in treatment(inside the bag) and the materials to store and deliver treatment.

Ice cream: Engineered cooling systems, insulated packing materials, and chemical preservatives allow a patient to eat a cool treat after her tonsils are removed.

Thermostat: Whether in a room, an oven, or a refrigerator, a thermostat is engineered to regulate the temperature of a space within a set range.

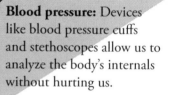

Blood pressure: Devices like blood pressure cuffs and stethoscopes allow us to analyze the body's internals without hurting us.

Bedpan: When you need to go, you need to go. The shape and feel of a bed pan may be created by an industrial designer, but engineers must decide whether it can be mass-produced in the desired material, shape, and cost.

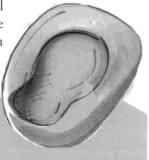

Antibacterial products: To reduce the chance of infection, antibacterial scrubs, washes, and even clothing have been engineered.

On a daily basis, I am surrounded by, utilize, and depend on engineered things to do my work. Even my relaxation activities have been affected by engineering.

Computer: In the old days, a computer took up a whole room, but engineers have created smaller, faster, and more versatile machines.

Picture frame: Displaying one's memories seems simple enough, but the range of choices in materials, colors, and styles are made possible by engineering minds.

Coat: We've come a long way from skinning an animal. Synthetic materials and machinery to make clothing more affordable are both products of engineering.

Chair: Modern office chairs have been improved by engineers. The wicking and form-fitting material was designed for comfort—and through mass-production methods, they are affordable for a personal home office.

Telephone: This device, and the complex network of cables and routers behind it, has been engineered over time to become more mobile (cordless and cell phones) and intelligent (call waiting, caller ID, and connection to the internet).

Gym bag: Working out requires special equipment and clothing to handle sweat and to give my feet bounce. An engineered waterproof, brightly colored, durable bag helps hold everything together.

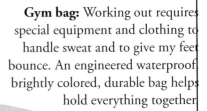

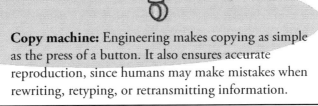

Copy machine: Engineering makes copying as simple as the press of a button. It also ensures accurate reproduction, since humans may make mistakes when rewriting, retyping, or retransmitting information.

While teaching engineering, I have found it tricky to clarify engineering from other disciplines, as engineers share traits and tasks with other professions. Because I can't narrow engineering into a neat package, I'll describe similarities and differences between engineering and other professions that are involved in "making things."

An engineer:

- **Must think creatively, like an artist**
  Engineers make sure that creations meet a need, while artists ensure that creations evoke the desired emotional response.[1]

- **Creates prototypes to test out ideas, like a technician**
  Engineers look at the larger project and formulate a plan to bring products not yet created into reality. Technicians must be expert in specific known technology (e.g., machining tools, wiring electonics, drawing devices, fixing car engines) in order to create or maintain existing products with the greatest accuracy and quality.

- **Considers how to mass-produce items**
  This aspect makes engineers different from an inventor or tinkerer, who makes just a few working products of a particular design.

- **Must consider cost and time constraints, like a businessperson**
  While engineers work on figuring out exactly how to make the idea into a reality, business counterparts concentrate on how they will sell the product, who will buy it, what it will cost, and what features it will have. Engineers sometimes successfully transition into business positions because they are grounded in physical reality and can make logical sense of data. These are skills needed for entrepreneurs and higher level management.[2]

- **Makes designs a reality**
  For example, civil engineers take care of all the steps needed to make an architect's ideas into real structures that humans can use. Mechanical engineers figure out how to make an industrial designer's product concepts into something that can be made with the desired features and quality.

- **Applies science and math**
  Electrical engineers use what is known about electricity to determine the right components for a task and how to connect them, while chemical engineers apply scientific knowledge to design materials with desired characteristics.

Things you can do

- Start seeing and sharing engineering's influence on everyday life.

- Treat each engineered product or system as a mystery to investigate. Use web and TV resources like *How Things Work* and *How It's Made* to find out more details.

- Talk about engineering as a viable career for kids, as you would a doctor, teacher, artist, or architect.

2: How Do Kids Prepare for Engineering?

I was becoming used to Quentin's way of putting things. What he was saying was that we had to start somewhere, either succeed or fail, and then build what we knew as we went along. ... Failure, after all, just added to our body of knowledge.
—Homer H. Hickman, Jr., in *October Sky*

It is possible that your kid is already blossoming into an engineer. The engineers I know share common traits that they developed as kids. Like sports stars, engineering masters develop their talents first through interests that capture their imaginations, then through play, and eventually through coaching by teachers, role models, and peers.

Engineers share what I refer to as eight basic traits. As with any profession, some people are stronger in some areas than others. From working with teachers, I find that many of these traits are desirable in general, both in school and for other professions. Developing these traits would be beneficial for any kid.

In this chapter, I'll share my story of ways that I developed the eight traits. Then we'll define the traits and why they are valuable for engineers. Through more biographical stories, we will explore how the traits are naturally developed in a kid's life and how they can be refined into the engineering design process—the way engineers turn ideas into reality to meet people's needs. Once you see the basic traits in your kids, you can help them develop into sophisticated problem solvers, and eventually engineers.

Itchy Fingers and Family Time: My Story

My own story is typical in some ways, but uniquely mine in others. The things I actually remember fondly are not obviously engineering-related. For example, though I was well behaved in front of others, I was constantly scolded by my father for having "itchy fingers" because I touched everything. I liked to feel the temperature and texture of materials, from the freezer units in the grocery store to the sugar dispenser on restaurant tables.

I also had a fascination with toilets. My parents noted that I insisted on going to the bathroom when we arrived at any new place (I asked Mom to take me) and again before we left (I wrangled Dad into taking me). While in the bathroom, I peered at how the toilet paper was dispensed and tried to figure out how the roll would be changed. I also tried to figure out how to use the stall door locks just by looking at them.

I was fortunate enough to have parents who took a vested interest in my education. They always phrased math problems in terms of puzzles, and through those, I discovered patterns and developed my skills. For example, when I was too bouncy to sleep, my mother had me distribute 35 quarters into 5 circles on a piece of paper (like the Easter bunny, I imagined). She had me first counting, then predicting, how many would be in each pile, which apparently had a similar effect on me as counting sheep has with other kids. I also liked feeling the coins in each hand as I manipulated them. Using math in this very physical way from a young age engaged my senses and helped me connect math to the physical world.

My parents both played games with me as well. Through *Mastermind*, *Battleship*, and *Pathfinder*, Dad helped me develop a problem-solving algorithm (strategy). Through *Monopoly* and *Life*, Mom had me practice my math skills by exchanging large bills into smaller ones to make change for a payment. *Sorry*, *Trouble*, and backgammon taught me to look ahead, realizing that one move earlier on could open or close opportunities in the future.

My parents also took me to science museums, zoos, and the park. We lived near Chicago at the time, which had incredible museums within close proximity to each other. My memories include the striking dinosaur displays at the Field Museum of Natural History, the eerie atmosphere of the Shedd Aquarium, and the coal mine and German submarine at the Museum of Science and Industry, which was my favorite. Closer to home, Tippecanoe Park had a real WWII plane among the swing sets and grassy fields, and kids could climb into it and sit in the cockpit. Through these experiences, I got to see the world and observe how things worked.

Life as a blossoming engineer is not always a cakewalk, and mine was no exception. I had two main struggles in my early years. Each might have derailed me, not just from engineering, but from school in general. Overcoming each helped me develop into a better engineer. Here's the story of the first struggle:

While in 2nd grade, I had a lot of problems in math. Though I had learned arithmetic skills from a young age, the timed tests were horrible for me. I consistently failed them, once getting only 4 out of 100 questions correct (yes, that's 4%). The teacher wrote a note to my parents declaring that I did not know how to do math.

Though my parents knew that timed tests were not the best way to evaluate math ability, they knew that I needed to master the test-taking requirements if that was how I was being graded. They approached the problem as other parents approached sports like basketball. First, they made sure I knew how to actually do the math, just as sports parents might have made sure that I knew how to make a basket.

Next, they had me practice math problems to help my performance on the actual task to be accomplished, just as sports parents might have their kids practice making baskets to ensure that a basket could be made every time in the heat of a live game. They tried a variety of practice drills—flash cards, worksheets with problems, and oral quizzes—but they found that a calculator programmed to give me random problems worked the best. Today, they probably would have used a computer program. I took that calculator everywhere. I did problems here and there whenever I was bored, whether in the car, waiting in line, or before church.

I apparently improved, because I don't remember failing any more math tests. In fact, by the end of 3rd grade, the teachers had me going to the 4th grade class to do more advanced math with them. My parents never believed that math was an innate gift, that some had and others didn't. When other parents would comment that I was lucky to be so talented in math, my parents simply responded that I worked hard. Just like Michael Jordan became a great basketball player because he practiced everyday, I became good at math because I practiced a lot of problems.

Practicing helped me later when I took the SAT, when I became an engineer, and whenever I ran into difficulties. My parents sent a clear message that hard work made me successful. Talent, they said, might help, but will only get you so far. It's the hard work, with whatever talent you do have, that they admired the most. So I learned to value that, too.

Eight Traits of an Engineer

The Necessary Four

These traits are usually (stereotypically) associated with engineering. All engineers must have them, and the typical engineering education expects them.

Interest in Science

Engineers need to understand how nature works, which is why physics, chemistry, and biology are required courses for many engineering specialties. Science methods are just as important as science knowledge. This includes developing logical observation and designing experiments to make sure design ideas are grounded in reality.[1]

Aptitude in Math

Engineers need to use logic, deal with abstract concepts, find patterns, and manipulate numbers, shapes, and space. Math develops these abilities, and mastery of these skills help engineers make use of nature, make decisions, and predict outcomes of actions.[1]

Perseverance

A good engineer ensures that work done leads to expected outcomes. Sticking to a problem until it is resolved is necessary because nothing ever is simple and projects always take longer than expected.

Problem Solving

Engineers efficiently tackle each problem encountered using a systematic approach (such as the Engineering Design Process) rather than random trial-and-error or purely "gut" decisions.

The Four That Enhance

These traits complement the Necessary Four. They are the reason engineering opens doors to other jobs. The more mastery engineers have of these, the more successful they tend to be.

Experience with Tools and Technology

The more engineers know the ins and outs of available tools and technology (e.g., materials, machinery, power sources, instruments, equipment, electronics, computers), the more success they have in turning ideas into reality.[2,3,4]

Ability to Think Spatially

Spatial abilities include rotating objects in one's head, placing objects in space, seeing their relations, and estimating distances. Research shows that these abilities are some of the best indicators for insightful research, patents, and general success in science and engineering.[5,6]

Creativity

The ability to imagine something that doesn't yet exist is central to an engineer's work.[7]

Ability to Communicate

Since engineers work in teams with people from different backgrounds (business, science, other engineering disciplines), written and oral communication about ideas, questions, and problems is essential.[1]

THE REWARD

Engineers emerge with a highly integrated understanding of the world and a solid core of practical knowledge and skills. Where others can only dream up products and systems to improve life, engineers have the ability to make them a reality.

How Kids Can Develop the Eight Traits

The next logical question is: How can you help your kid develop these traits so this wonderful thing called engineering can be an option? The most obvious way would be to sit your loved one down and say, "OK, let's get better at… math, science, communication…" But your kid may be developing these traits anyway, through his or her normal activities or interests. Encouraging those tendencies may be a subtler, more effective way to help develop these traits.

Humans in general have some engineering tendencies. After all, the day someone decided to make a shelter rather than search around for the perfect cave was a big day for engineering. Another engineering moment was when humans realized that a rock could be deliberately shaped into a point. They realized that they didn't have to rely only on searching for rocks randomly shaped by nature. It shouldn't be surprising if you see engineering abilities and tendencies in your kids. They are human, after all.

I saw the angel in the marble and carved until I set him free.

—Michelangelo

Each of us has our own engineering moments, those times where we either accept the world as it is presented to us or decide to use our brains and experiences to make our lives a little better. An engineer chooses the latter approach.

Artificial Legs: My first introduction to engineering

The second struggle I had came from my birth defect. I was born missing some bones in my leg and ankle and had to have many operations starting at 1½ years old. At the age of 5, my foot was removed and I was fitted with a prosthesis (artificial leg). So that I would better understand my condition, my parents bought me a human anatomy book, which I loved to read. This helped me develop the *science* trait.

My disability was never a secret. With each new grade and each new school, my mother arranged for me to stand up in front of the class, show them my prosthesis, and explain what it was and how I got it. That was when I answered questions from my new classmates, and how we set up a way to talk about my disability *(communication)*.

When I was 13, I apparently got surly. While some surliness might have been normal for a teenager, it was enough for my father to comment that I was "being grumpy a lot." I complained about my leg not fitting properly; in fact, it was downright painful. Since I was growing rapidly due to puberty, the leg either was too tight or, when I adjusted it, became too loose and slammed into the bottom of the prosthesis with each step. As a result, I was constantly in pain.

This was a problem my father felt he could tackle. Together, we figured out a fastening system that used ski boot buckles rather than shoelaces. This system allowed me to quickly adjust the tightness of the prosthesis and wouldn't slip to a different size by accident *(problem solving, tools and technology, spatial skills, creativity)*.

This was my first taste of how to engineer a solution. Engineering suddenly meant not having to accept the world as it was handed to me. This project was only the start of engineering to improve life. Later, I worked on projects that would help other engineers design jet engines more efficiently, warehouse workers track inventory, laboratory chemists design materials with the desired characteristics, and factory employees ensure quality products. My engineer husband and I joined forces to make a prosthetic swimming foot that I can use on beach vacations and whil scuba diving, showing that engineering is useful for both work and play.

My story has some similarities with other engineers'. Their experiences developed the traits that helped them become successful engineers. As you'll see below, each story is unique yet timeless. The names have been changed, but the stories are real.

Different or unique? Lynne's story

Lynne was used to being an outsider. An only child in a military family, she lived abroad for a good portion of her life. Moving to different schools and living in places like Korea and Hawaii, she often had to figure out how to fit in. She did things with the other kids such as swimming at the beach, hanging out with neighborhood kids, and playing in the band, but she still enjoyed activities she did alone, like figuring out jigsaw puzzles *(spatial skills)* and reading. She particularly liked poetry in all its manifestations, including pop music, rap, and jazz.

When computers came to Lynne's school, she enjoyed figuring out how to program them *(problem solving)*. She realized that the logical skills she honed in *mathematics* helped her create programs to help and entertain herself and her friends *(creativity)*. In college, she decided to go into engineering because she was good at *science* and math, and because she wanted to learn more about the computer as a machine, not just program it.

However, unlike many of her classmates, Lynne had not built her own computer or even worked with electronics. At first, she wondered if she belonged in the field because she seemed so behind, but she later realized that everyone has to learn about technology and its tools sometime. She told herself, "If I didn't know it in the womb, I can ask." This helped her feel less embarrassed about having less knowledge than her classmates at the outset *(perseverance)*.

With all the challenges she faced early in her life, Lynne learned not to stress in unfamiliar or even uncomfortable situations. This foundation of believing in her own intelligence, working with people, and being comfortable with the unknown helped her become an expert in the new field of internet networking.

Late bloomer makes good: Roy's story

Roy was a squirrely child, literally. He spent every moment he could in the woods, watching the squirrels scurry about, hearing the birds warn each other of his approach, and even catching sight of an occasional deer. When he wasn't stalking in the woods with his bow and arrow and later his BB gun *(spatial skills)*, he was rounding up friends to make a tree house or to explore deeper in the ravine near his house *(communication)*. The woods were his scientific observatory and experimental ground, where he learned about biology, physics, and material properties.

After his parents divorced when he was young, Roy found the woods as his sanctuary more and more. When school started, he had a hard time adjusting. He struggled with math and spelling, in particular, but excelled in art class *(spatial skills)*.

In high school, he spent hours after school making jewelry *(creativity, tools and technology)*. When his school offered the opportunity to take ground school classes to train for aviation, he jumped at the chance. Though money was tight, Roy's father pulled together money for him to take flight lessons as well. Finally, it made sense to Roy why he had to learn *math*—to do weight calculations so he wouldn't fall out of the sky—and spell right—to leave flight plans and records so others knew what he was doing *(communication)*.

Because there are so many things to remember, aviators have a series of checklists to consult at each phase of their flight. This habit of making and consulting a checklist helped Roy with his schoolwork *(problem solving)*, which he wanted to improve since he realized he needed to go to college to become a pilot. Later, Roy decided that creating new things was a more rewarding career for him than flying, and he became an engineer. Math and spelling were still a challenge, but he used the structured habits developed in flight training to get his bachelor's and then master's degree in engineering *(perseverance)*.

After years of working on a variety of products, Roy struck out on his own and started his own engineering product design company, and even filed a few patents for his inventions.

Confused or creative? Al's story

Young Al was sickly in his early years, contracting a disease that resulted in persistent earaches. At the age of twelve, he lost his hearing in one ear. However, when he entered school, hearing seemed to be the least of his worries. Teachers called him "confused," criticized his atrocious handwriting, and were frustrated trying to keep him still and focused on the assignments at hand. Even his father wondered about his intelligence, saying rather unkind things about his abilities.

However, his mother tutored him and encouraged him to explore the world around him. She often had to make sure that he ate properly while he was doggedly pursuing a problem (*perseverance, problem solving*). Although he accidentally burned down the family barn once, she still helped him set up a lab at home to run experiments (*science*).

Al read avidly, learning everything he could from the books he could obtain. He was notorious for taking apart anything that captured his imagination. He developed a system for laying out the parts so that he could reverse the process and put the device back together again (*tools and technology, spatial skills*).

Eventually, he made a living engineering new inventions using the latest scientific phenomenon of electromagnetism: they included the phonograph and electric light bulb (creativity). We know him today as Thomas Alva Edison.

Traditional woman, untraditional directions:
Lillian Moller Gilbreth's story

Lillian was one of many children. Because her mother was ill, she stayed home to care for her and was home schooled. She didn't enter school until she was nine, but once there, she relished the opportunity to learn. She particularly took to literature and music (*perseverance, communication*). Her father didn't believe in college for women, but she convinced him to let her attend (*problem solving, creativity*). There, she studied modern languages and philosophy, preparing herself to become an English teacher. She even continued on to graduate school but had to drop out when she became ill.

Returning home, she eventually received her master's degree in literature. Once again, she convinced her father to let her travel. This was when she met Frank, who would later become her husband. Frank Gilbreth was a working man who made a reputation for himself in efficient methods of construction. Ready to explore new areas, he was convinced that by parnering with Lillian, they could do great things. After Frank and Lillian were married, they raised twelve children. Lillian learned more about construction from Frank and became interested in the human aspects of work She believed that knowing more about human psychology would help her contribute to the problems yet to be solved, so she completed a doctorate in psychology (*science*). Together, they filmed workers, figuring out how they could do their tasks more efficiently and safely.

When a surgeon asks for a scalpel and the nurse efficiently provides the right one, you see an example of their work. Training for touch typing on the current QWERTY typewriter layout was improved by them, using colors and feel-based methods. Sadly, Frank died at the height of their work.

With the help of her children and her own determination, Lillian carried on the business and became a leader in the new field of scientific management, which turned into industrial engineering. She trained industrialists from around the world to create more efficient and user-friendly environments, but also designed environments and tools for non-industrial settings. The efficiency kitchen was her brainchild, where everything was within arm's reach, refrigerator doors had shelves, and the garbage pail could be opened with one foot (*spatial skills*). Industrial engineering uses observation, quantitative rasoning (*math*), and human considerations to make work safer and more efficient. Lillian hoped it would allow people more time to have meaningful pursuits, but engineers saw her as a great engineeer. You can read more about her in the books *Cheaper by the Dozen* and *Belles on Their Toes*.

The Engineering Design Process

A system for problem solving and perseverance

Now let's look at how you can help kids with engineering traits start thinking like engineers. They can solve problems they care about using the Engineering Design Process.

Teachers I work with tell me that many kids today are afraid of failure, specifically not succeeding on the very first try. With schools shutting down when students don't test well, kids feel the pressure of not getting the right answer. However, engineering is an iterative process that does not expect success in the first few tries. In fact, a smart engineer expects that the first solution will be less than perfect and can always be improved.

Teachers have informed me that the Engineering Design Process has helped kids feel more comfortable with "failure." With it, they help kids adopt the positive habit of "If at first you don't succeed, try, try again" that is so essential for engineering.

STEM education standards speak of "The Engineering Design Process," as if there is just one. When I talk with engineers about "The" process, they cock their heads and look quizzically at me. I get it; I had the same reaction. As engineers, we were never were taught an explicit process, but we all do an iterative one based on perseverance, prototyping, and logic. Every K-12 engineering curriculum seems to have its own process—some even encompass up to 12 steps! At the heart, though, are three actions (analyze, design, build) and two touch points (need, constraint).

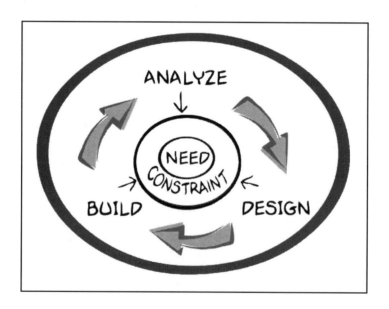

Here's an example from my introduction to engineering class: build toy furniture from spaghetti that can hold ten times its own weight. At first, this seems impossible, so we guide students through the Engineering Process. First they *analyze* what forces must be handled: A chair's legs must handle the weight of whatever is placed on them. But spaghetti is not strong under this compression force, as you may have noticed when you pull a strand from the box and accidentally push it into the counter.

After doing some research, students discover that arranging the pieces into small triangles called trusses can create a stronger structure. They find a truss *design* that might work, and then they *build* a small truss to test out the idea. After testing, they *analyze* the results—it stands! Yay! But now there's a new problem. The furniture leg must be longer than a strand of spaghetti. How will they solve that problem? Easy. Use the Engineering Design Process again: analyze, design, then build and repeat, checking each time if the new creation (prototype) helps meet the *need* (make functional furniture) under the given *constraints* (spaghetti only).

In short, the Engineering Design Process breaks down need into a series of small, manageable problems. Doing this makes a seemingly impossible task more manageable. For kids, this can be used when building a tall tower of blocks, figuring out how to move wood from the house to the forest to make a tree house, or planning out a banquet so all the food comes out on time. Typical engineering projects use it when collecting clean water, mass-producing a new cookie product, or flying to the moon.

The Engineering Design Process, if started early with simple projects, can develop habits and perspectives that can help kids become great engineers. Let's look at a famous real-life example.

Rocket Boys in October Sky: An Engineering Design Process Story

In the non-fiction book *October Sky*, a group of boys in a coal-mining town started with a desire: They were inspired by the Russian satellite Sputnik to build rockets. Fueled by the science fiction stories they read, they wanted to see what they could do for the space effort. The book was made into a movie in 1999, but some of the details of how the boys developed the eight traits by following the Engineering Design Process were left out of the film.

While reading the story, you can see how the boys had the burning *need* to make a rocket that could fly high. They were *constrained* by materials, money, and even space, since they were not allowed to work anywhere owned by the coal company—which was pretty much the whole town.

They zeroed in on their solution by cycling through the Engineering Design Process (though they didn't realize it). Each problem they encountered (how to design and construct the casement and nozzle, how to mix the fuel, how to measure the height, and even how to conduct the launch) required them to learn a bit more *(analyze),* whether that was Newton's Laws of Motion or the chemistry of black powder. With this knowledge, they conceived, drew, and modeled ideas *(design)*. They then hammered, bent, and fastened materials to create prototypes based on these ideas *(build)*. They often created multiple models with the same design to rigorously test their ideas *(analyze)*.

With each success, they had to learn more such as trigonometry and later calculus in order to quantitatively *analyze* how high their rockets went. Each test result gave them more information about how to better meet their need, whether the test succeeded or failed.

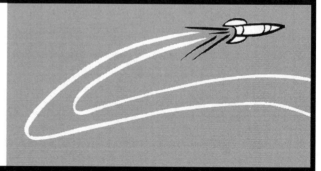

By continuing their efforts using the Engineering Design Process, they developed their *tools and technology* experience by learning to solder, weld, draft, and machine as well as exploring different metals, glues, and chemicals for fuel. Shaping and designing the rocket, planning launches, and measuring the height helped them develop *spatial skills*, and they constantly had to use their *creativity* and *communication* skills to solve the technical problems as well as all the public relations issues they had with neighbors, teachers, and their own parents.

These traits proved to help them in life. They went on to win the National Science Fair and eventually made their way to college. Four of the six boys became engineers, with one ending up at NASA, designing real spacecraft!

Pulling It All Together

From these stories, you can see some trends:

- Each of these engineers started with their basic interests: tinkering, puzzling, creating, or analyzing. From there, they formed habits that helped develop the essential engineering traits.

- Each had time to play, read, and otherwise pursue interests through formal activities such as clubs and courses or informal activities such as hobbies, toys, and games.

- All had the support of one or both parents, in the form of resources, space, time, advice, knowledge, money, or habits of mind.

- Each found ways to learn more about the world around them through reading, taking things apart, and experiencing and seeing how things worked through sports, chores, or hobbies.

- For most, some of the eight traits came later in life. Each required constant effort to learn and improve.

When taken together, these stories show that we all have the capacity and potential to do engineering to some degree. In short, all humans can engineer.

Things you can do

- While supporting your kid in his or her current interests, point out the engineering traits he or she is developing and how they can be used to engineer solutions to problems your kid cares about.

- Talk about developing and practicing technical skills (math, science, tools and technology, and spatial skills). Avoid using words like "gift" or "talent," which give the impression that either a kid "has it" or doesn't.

- Encourage your kid to follow up with questions or challenges, using the Engineering Design Process to help him or her get started and to overcome obstacles along the way.

- Celebrate times that your kid "sticks" to something, regardless of the results. This could be as simple as making a "certificate of achievement" or making a favorite snack to share while reminiscing about the challenge that was tackled. Talk positively about what your kid learned from the experience or what future projects could follow.

3. What Would My Kid Do as an Engineer?

In fact, deep down I had concluded that it was the main business of humankind to build, to be technologically creative. Literature I felt in my bourgeois heart of hearts, was commentary upon life, while engineering was the stuff of life itself.

—Samuel Florman in *The Civilized Engineer*

For some kids, engineering is a calling once they discover it. They are amazed that they can go to school to learn how to do more with their beloved interests. Others go into engineering as more of a default—they like math and science but also want to use or apply those subjects. Or though they love English literature or history, they are not really sure if they want to pursue careers related to those fields. Kids who entertain the thought of going into engineering often have a strong practical bent. "What can we do with this?" is on the tip of their tongues when they learn something new. But what kinds of jobs would a graduating engineer do?

First, it is important to realize that there are different types of engineering. The one that is best for your kid really depends on what he or she finds interesting. A kid who likes to build or explore buildings, climb on bridges or structures, figure out bus schedules, or create pools and rivers in the sandbox may be a budding civil engineer. A future electrical or computer engineer may start as a kid who is fascinated with electronics or lights, plays with computers, sets up home entertainment systems for fun, or figures out how to get the microwave, answering machine, or cell phone to work as desired. One who plays with windup toys, heats and cools materials to change them (e.g., Shrinky Dinks or Sculpey clay), or fixes or improves the design of household objects may become a mechanical engineer.

But what your kid majors in doesn't always translate into a specific job title. Problems today are complex, so multiple perspectives are important in solving them. An engineering education simply arms students with a body of knowledge and approaches to solve a part of a problem. In fact, many engineering job titles do not directly correlate to the majors who fill them. "Test engineer" and "packaging engineer" are actual job titles in industry, but there are no such majors. Instead, an engineer with the required skill set would fill those positions.

WORKING TOGETHER TO TURN IDEAS INTO REALITY

If a company wants to create a new product—for example, a healthier cookie—several different experts come together to turn the idea into a reality. Some aspects require engineering knowledge and skills. Other aspects require very specific scientific knowledge, so scientists are required. Business aspects require an understanding of people as well as the ability to make decisions based on market data.

Product Idea: Comes from anyone from various backgrounds and experience.

Business Marketing Analyst: Determines the demand for the cookie ("Will anyone buy it if we make it?").

Food Scientist: Figures out the recipe to make the cookie to get the expected nutritional content and taste requirements.

Chemist: Figures out other chemicals needed to produce and preserve the cookie.

Chemical Engineer: Scales up the recipe generated by the scientists, determines the chemical processes needed, and adjusts the recipe as needed.

Mechanical Engineer: Figures out how to design the equipment necessary to produce the cookie.

Civil Engineer: Determines the building or structural support needed for the factory. Works with architects who determine how the space should be laid out and used.

Electrical Engineer: Figures out the electrical components needed for the equipment.

Test Engineer (in Quality Assurance): Ensures that the cookies meet specified quality requirements by creating processes to sample and equipment to test.

Manufacturing Engineer: Figures out how to optimize the manufacturing process using machines, procedures, or overall organization. Also solves problems found after the cookie has been launched.

Packaging Engineer: Figures out how the cookie will be packaged, both individually and when shipped in bulk.

Business Marketing and Sales: Launches the cookie to the public for purchase (advertising, sales visits, promotional deals).

From College Majors to Industry

Many teachers ask me to suggest which engineering fields their kids should consider and what a typical day would look like for them. Sadly, I have difficulties answering them succinctly. First, there are many different engineering disciplines, ranging from broad topics such as mechanical, chemical, or electrical engineering to specific ones like petroleum, nuclear, or even ocean engineering. Then, no matter what students major in, they usually are employed in a wide variety of jobs during their career. It's enough to get confusing, and it promotes the idea that a kid must decide on the specific job and major to pursue very early on.

When I advise high school and college students, I try to give them a framework to understand engineering majors as well as engineering jobs, so they don't get confused by the various specialties. This is particularly important when I deal with students who aren't really sure what they want to do "for the rest of their lives." I try to help them keep their options open while they discover their strengths, improve their weaknesses, and find out how they can contribute to the world.

Positions in each of these industries have various levels of routine, which makes it difficult to describe a "typical day." For example, when I was working as a consultant, I would sometimes report to work in the office and program weighing machines for customers. Another day, though,

What Do Engineers Do?

If "work" is how you get paid for a living, following the money can help you see what an engineer does. Three main industries I have found that pay engineers are:

- *Government Agencies:* Here, the money comes from taxpayers. Projects depend on the government body that employs them. These include local city governments that employ engineers to design and manage sanitation, local street maintenance, traffic control, and public transportation. State and federal government agencies such as NASA and the Departments of Transportation, Energy, and Natural Resources, employ engineers to regulate industries that affect society's resources, such as energy, water, or environment. They also develop public works projects such as highways and bridges and provide for national security through military equipment development, internet security, and access to outer space. The military itself is one of the largest employers of engineers in the nation. The character Q from the James Bond movies would be a British government-employed engineer!

- **_Manufacturing Industries:_** Here, I use the term "manufacturing" broadly, meaning any industry that earns its money from products that are sold. These products can be anything; phones, computer software, soap products, cars, home repair materials, food products, etc. Most people think of these types of jobs at companies such as Apple, Xerox, Tesla, ZipCar, Proctor and Gamble, Target, and Medtronic.

- **_Consulting Services:_** Here, the money comes from offering engineering know-how to others. In this case, a consulting engineer may be working on a product that will eventually make money, but the engineer will be paid whether the product is a success of not. The engineering consultant's commodity is his or her knowledge, skills, and abilities required for particular stages in the Engineering Design Process. A consultant may be brought on to a project to do specific technical tasks because the engineers on staff at a manufacturing company are too busy to handle them or because a special expertise is needed. For example, a small biomedical company may hire a mechanical engineering consultant with expertise in plastic part design, an electrical engineer for help with GPS technology, a computer engineer to program a particular functionality, or a chemical engineer who specializes in a new bioplastic material.

Positions in each of these industries have various levels of routine, which makes it difficult to describe a "typical day." For example, when I was working as a consultant, I would sometimes report to work in the office and program weighing machines for customers. Another day, though, I might have to be in a meeting with a client to determine the requirements for the new machines we would be delivering. Yet another day might be co-opted by an emergency call from a customer whose computer system froze up, causing them to restart the system. Sometimes I would report directly to the factory and install, tweak, or debug the systems or train the employees on how to use the system.

And this brings up another aspect of engineering jobs. Though many of us use our specific technical expertise in our daily jobs, a good portion of many engineers' jobs includes project management. Engineers are often put in charge of the project. Why? They know how to figure out what's technically possible, and they know how to manage the work-arounds needed to get the desired outcome. Thus, sometimes part of my daily routine is to check the progress of the project, ensure that the other players are on track, and update the client on the milestones. So a really successful engineer needs technical know-how, big-picture vision, and people skills.

What the engineering workplace looks like is equally varied, often depending on the size of the employer. In the United States, the types of companies that usually employ engineers include big corporate ones like 3M, General Mills, or Google who employ on the order of 10,000 people or more; medium-sized companies whose employees number in the thousands; small companies (in the hundreds); and startup companies (as few as a handful of people). Each has its own scope of work, requirements for its engineers, and level of formal or casual work environment. In short, there is no "typical" engineering job. The day in a life of an engineer can range from suits in a corporate cubicle to a T-shirt in the back of a garage.

What Do Engineers Major In?

Some students go to college wanting to specialize in alternative energy or biomedical technologies. As a result, they believe that they need to major in specialized areas such as environmental engineering or biomedical engineering. But depending on what aspects they are interested in, they may actually be better off majoring in a more "generic" engineering field such as mechanical or electrical engineering and taking on projects focused on their specific areas of interest. This will give them a technical expertise and skill set that will allow them to play a stronger role in a broader range of applications.

I have to confess that my foundational approach to engineering majors is influenced by my own education. I went to Princeton University's engineering program, which has historically limited itself to just a few types of engineering majors. It makes sense; some of specific engineering areas such as petroleum or nuclear focus on specific new technology. Today, many of these areas have become specialties within one of the basic engineering fields. Sticking to the basics can give a longer-term perspective.

The "Big Four"

Which are the "basic" engineering fields? Let's take a look at fields by the most popular degrees earned, using a recent analysis of the engineering majors recognized by the Accreditation Board for Engineering and Technology (ABET).

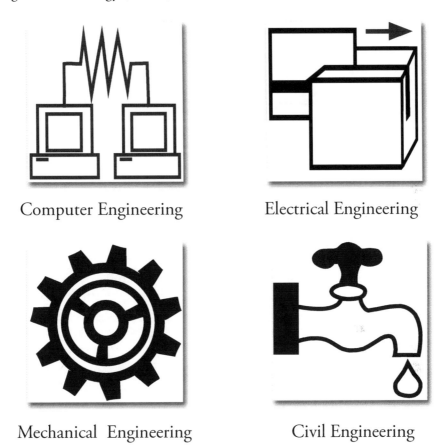

Computer Engineering   Electrical Engineering

Mechanical Engineering   Civil Engineering

About two-thirds of engineering bachelor's degrees earned are in the "Big Four" majors.[1] Why? These prepare students for the **Computer**, **Electrical**, and **Mechanical** components that support any number of industries. Our cookie example showed how the food industry can use these disciplines. Other industries include communications (e.g., cell phones, television, radio), appliances (microwaves, refrigerators, washers, and dryers), household products (furniture, wheelchairs, flashlights) and specialty products (equipment for hospitals, sports teams, or law enforcement). They also support the nation's **Civil** infrastructure not only in large structures (bridges, tunnels, buildings) but also transit, sanitation, and energy management. Basically, whatever you see in the engineered world (i.e., what you learned in Chapter 1) has at least one of these components in the "Big Four." This is why most of the jobs are in these areas.

The "Middle Four"

Aerospace Engineering

Biomedical Engineering

Chemical Engineering

Industrial or Manufacturing Engineering

About 20% of engineering bachelor's degrees are in the "Middle Four." These are more specialized, but these engineers often work in teams with others from the "Big Four" areas.

- **Aerospace** engineers cover the design of structures, propulsion, and control of aeronautical vehicles (e.g., airplanes, gliders, high altitude balloons) and space vehicles. They may also work on ground vehicles to improve their aerodynamics (e.g., reducing drag). They work closely with mechanical engineers to provide more aerospace-specific expertise on particular mechanical aspects, such as structural strength of materials and designs, vibration, thermodynamics (temperature control as well as engine combustion), and control systems (intelligence and monitoring systems, such as autopilot or cruise control).

- **Biomedical** engineers coordinate the design of materials, devices, drugs, and diagnostic equipment used in medical fields. They work with a team of engineers, depending on what the product is: chemical engineers for materials or drugs; mechanical and electrical engineers for devices and diagnostic equipment.

- **Chemical** engineers work with anything involving chemicals, such as fuels, commercial chemicals (e.g., cleaners, pesticides), food and drugs, and materials (e.g., ceramics, metals, composites).

- **Industrial/Manufacturing** engineers work to make the manufacturing process more efficient and reliable by determining how the factory is physically laid out, how the equipment is designed, and how work is done by humans and machines to reduce injuries while increasing safety and performance.

The "Smaller Ten" and Specialty Disciplines

Agricultural
Engineering

Architectural
Engineering

Environmental
Engineering

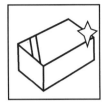
Materials
Engineering

Mining
Engineering

Nuclear
Engineering

Petroleum
Engineering

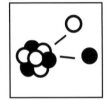
Engineering
Physics

Engineering
Management

Ocean
Engineering

The other 15% of engineering degrees include the "Smaller Ten" and specialty engineering fields. Many times, these are part of the other engineering disciplines. For example, architectural engineering may be concentrated within civil engineering; materials and petroleum engineering may be housed with chemical engineering; environmental engineering may be housed in either civil or chemical engineering, depending on the university's expertise and focus; and agricultural, mining, and ocean engineering may be associated with mechanical engineering.

Pulling It All Together

Learning about engineering is really only the beginning. The engineering traits a person develops while young can open a lot of other options. Take my sister. She learned mathematics from my parents and read my science books, but she also competed in Science Olympiad and MathCounts and ran a "fix it" shop for the house, fixing broken items like umbrellas or cases, selecting the right glues or putties to make the item seem like new. Later, I taught her how to use HTML to create web pages from scratch. In some ways, she developed her engineering traits more than I did.

But my sister decided to major in English and is now a professional writer—editing, blogging, and writing short stories and novels. Her engineering traits are not wasted in her life. In the summers of her college years, she made extra income by selling miniature 1/12th scale food for dollhouse collectors. She combined her writing talents with her web programming abilities to create a web page that connected her with customers as far away as England. In a tight recession, she secured a job in editing science textbooks because, unlike other English majors, she enjoyed and understood science. When she was editing web-based manuscripts, the programmers were delighted that she knew HTML and could make the changes herself and help relieve their packed schedules. When she worked in the library, she taught herself some Perl search commands to make her life easier. At home, she is able to handle a lot of repairs, investments, and purchases with a tech-savvy eye.

For those who do major in engineering, engineering provides entrance to other fields such as management, finance, marketing, non-profit work, entrepreneurship, or something completely different. For each of the people I know who left engineering, engineering has provided a valuable knowledge and skill set for their new position or provides them a way to make a reasonable income while pursuing less lucrative interests. For them, engineering was not an end goal; it simply opened the door to more options.

Things you can do

- *Parents:* If you have family, friends, or neighbors who are engineers, ask them for field trips to their work, objects they work with, or conversations with your kid about what they do. Ask them to share how what they do affects (or can affect) your kid's life.

- *Teachers:* Talk with engineering societies (e.g., Society of Women Engineers, IEEE, ASME, ASCE, ACM) about outreach activities. Explicitly connect kids' excitement of doing activities with the engineering traits, school subjects, and everyday life.

- Provide kits (chemical, electronic, mechanics) to allow your kid to play with the technology and see what is exciting and interesting.

- Notice and share different engineering results seen in the news, magazines, TV shows, or movies.

- Take advantage of free "behind the scenes" tours of facilities such as water treatment plants, factories, or malls and amusement parks.

4: Who Says My Kid Can't Do Engineering?

*I'm not going to limit myself just because people
won't accept the fact that I can do something else.*
—Dolly Parton

With all the hype about needing more engineers for national competitiveness, you might be surprised that some people express concern or even outright skepticism about your kid's ability to become an engineer. This discouragement might not be obvious and often has roots in reasons unrelated to the eight traits. For example, as a woman, Lillian Moller Gilbreth faced difficulties in being recognized as an engineering expert. As her children wrote in her biography, *Belles on Their Toes*:

> The financial outlook became, if anything, even worse than Mother had expected.
> The big firms declined to renew their motion study contracts. Various reasons
> were offered. They boiled down to the belief that, while Mother might know the
> theory of motion study, no woman could handle the technical details of the job or
> command the respect and cooperation of shop foremen and workers.

Other discouragements are far more obvious and worse, can be internally adopted by the child. Thomas Edison, now recognized as person with dyslexia, recalled, "My teachers say I'm addled . . . my father thought I was stupid, and I almost decided I must be a dunce."

Even well-meaning adults may do a disservice by trying to eliminate career options for kids early. These adults—teachers, parents, relatives—mistakenly believe that being weak in an engineering trait such as math eliminates engineering from a kid's future, so they don't even mention engineering as a possible career, despite strengths in other traits. What they don't realize is that kids are highly adaptive and resourceful; they can use one trait, such as spatial skills, to bide time while they develop other traits such as math ability. In fact, kids achieve more than expected if they are driven by a need they care about.

Unfortunately, this tendency to weed kids out of engineering early can end up segregating them by other characteristics, such as gender, race, or socioeconomic status. Since engineering is important for national economic competitiveness, a better strategy would be to figure out how to encourage engineering traits in all kids, rather than trying to identify an engineering elite. To truly tap our full national potential, it is important to realize that engineering traits are sometimes underdeveloped because of lack of exposure, not lack of ability. When the root cause is addressed, amazing things can happen.

In this chapter we will explore some of the most common issues I have encountered regarding kids' engineering potential. First are the facts I have gathered from published research and my work with teachers, parents, college students, and children. We then discuss some underlying aspects as they relate to engineering and consider what you, as a parent or teacher, can do for the kids you care about.

Be forewarned: we will discuss some touchy subjects, and I apologize ahead of time if I accidentally offend. I only hope that this is the first of many honest discussions that will help all kids pursue engineering.

Math Challenges

Math is an important tool in the engineer's toolbox. However, I know plenty of engineers (including myself) who faced challenges in math class. If your kid isn't classified as a "math genius," it doesn't mean engineering is impossible.

One thing to remember is that mathematics is a very broad field. Most people think of numbers and operations (addition, division, etc.) when they think of math. But in reality, mathematics also involves defining and manipulating numbers, shapes, and space; finding patterns in numbers, shapes, and procedures; and using logic to figure out how solving one problem gives insight into seemingly different problems (also known as abstracting concepts).

The dominant view in American culture is that math is an innate talent or gift. In other countries, math ability is considered something you improve with practice and hard work.[1] In fact, many of my international students were far more comfortable with doing math than writing an essay in English. Why? To quote the movie *Mean Girls:* "Math is the same in every country."

An engineer comfortable with math can be more efficient in making reasonable decisions and can better predict outcomes of actions.

Things you can do

- *Make it physical:* Some kids have problems "seeing" what the math problem is asking. Using props can help them "see" the numbers and operations. Use coins or candies to illustrate addition, subtraction, multiplication, and division. Use play money to show how "borrowing" is really "trading in" a larger bill ($10) for a bunch of smaller ones ($1) that can be used in subtraction.

- *Make it meaningful:* Reveal everyday math problems like in the book *Math Curse*. Before starting calculations, describe the equation as a short story: instead of 5=x+3, say "If my favorite dessert costs $5, and I have $3 in my wallet, how much do I need to borrow from my friend?" Putting the problem in context creates a purpose and enhances abstraction skills. You can also do this by drawing pictures to illustrate word problems. Use pencil so that the picture can be modified as the problem is read. This is similar to an artist sketching and modifying images until the final one is realized.

- *Practice the process of problem solving:* Encourage the idea that many "drafts" of the solution are required. Have a stack of scratch paper to try out solution ideas, using a new sheet for each new problem. This physical separation of thoughts is helpful for visual and kinesthetic learners.

- *Emphasize finding a procedure for solving the problem:* With each homework assignment, help your kid create a "standard operating procedures" notebook that can be used every time he or she forgets how to solve a type of problem. This increases accuracy, relieves anxiety, and emphasizes that the process is what's important, not the numeric answer.

Spatial Challenges

The ability to see and manipulate things in his or her head makes an engineer more efficient in solving real-life problems. But spatial thinking is a challenge, even for some engineers. If your kid has problems with reading blueprints, using a map, or estimating sizes, engineering is still

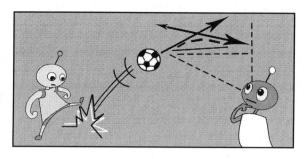

possible. One thing to remember is that spatial skills have been improved with practice, even for older college students.[2] In fact, I once knew a woman with horrible visiospatial skills who worked with her family's catering business every summer, packing up leftovers for clients. Eventually, she was able to figure out which plastic container to use for any food she had to pack with amazing accuracy. With practice, her mind was able to squish products like potato salad into a completely different shape.

A few fun ways to practice:

- *Games:* Tangrams, Zoob
- *Toys:* LEGOs, Flexeez, K'nex
- *Video games:* Bejeweled, Color Junction, Tetris, World of Goo
- *Art:* Drawing, sewing, cooking, photography, sculpting, wood shop, jewelry making, theatre
- *Athletics:* Ball sports (basketball, soccer, football), paddle sports (tennis, softball, baseball, hockey, lacrosse), positioning activities (skating, biking, skiing)
- *Nature endeavors:* Orienteering, geo-caching, archery, target practice, climbing

Everyday ways:
- Navigating with a map
- Packing leftovers or the car
- Designing storage space
- Building shelves and frames

Classroom activities:
- Technical drawing
- Construction projects
- Physically acting out concepts

Another thing to remember is that kids with spatial difficulties often have good verbal skills (and vice versa). Put physical items in their hands and have them describe what they see. Have them talk about the geometric features (holes, slanted lines, curves), realizing that they are landmarks from which they can go "up," "left," or "forward." Have them put their fingers on these same features as they are represented in blueprint views, and have them use the words they generate to move their finger to the right places on the blueprint.

This helps the brain correspond the drawn geometric features to the real thing. Use this same verbal technique to describe complex operations like spinning, flipping, or even modifying the shape. Studies with preschoolers show that an increase of spatial words seem to increase spatial test performance.[3]

Learning Disabilities

Learning disabilities are conditions that cause difficulty in learning, remembering, or concentrating. Commonly known disabilities are dyslexia, dyscalculia, dysgraphia, dispraxia, attention deficit hyperactivity disorder (ADHD), and autism. Undiagnosed, learning disabilities are sometimes misperceived as lack of effort or lack of maturity of the student. They are most noticeable in school when kids have difficulty in reading, writing, spelling, doing math, using money, telling time, or distinguishing symbols, or in staying still, organized, or focused.[4,5]

Why bother with these kids if learning is so difficult? Interestingly, some of these "disabilities" can be "superpowers" in engineering. Studies are being done to see if people with Asperger's do well in engineering because of their attention to detail,[6] while those with dyslexia (who see "b" and "d" as the same) often have advantages when it comes to spatial skills. Kids with ADHD have difficulties with tests but are often a wellspring of ideas. Since they multitask so much, they are able to keep options open, and once interested, they are usually tenacious. Imagine what they could do armed with engineering! Many become entrepreneurs.

While coping, kids with learning disabilities learn first-hand that perseverance and creative problem solving bring success. Developing effective learning strategies minimizes the effects of learning disabilities and helps the brain make new connections. Coping strategies can develop engineering traits, since they both involve connecting language and symbols with physical reality. Civilizations have known the value of this for years. As the Chinese saying goes: "I hear and I forget. I see and I remember. I do and I understand." Some of my engineering friends exhibit ADHD, autistic, or dyslexic characteristics; a learning disability doesn't have to be a barrier to engineering.

Things you can do

Strategies that pull ideas and thoughts into the physical world help exercise all parts of the brain and facilitate "seeing" ideas.

Auditory: Need to hear information
- Read notes out loud
- Talk through ideas with others
- Use word association to memorize

Visual: Need to see information
- Create flashcards
- Take color-coded notes
- Make outlines, diagrams, or lists

Kinesthetic: Need to use body to remember
- Get his or her hands on things
- Take field trips
- Do role playing
- Study with background music

Gender Considerations

With women comprising only 11% of practicing engineers and less than 20% of engineering majors, there are significantly fewer women pursing engineering than men. However, fewer men are attending college, a necessary step on the road to engineering. How you approach your kid about engineering is different depending on your kid's gender.

If you have a girl:

Girls' low representation is not due to ability: recent studies show that girls do just as well as boys in science and math. Moreover, they show similar levels of interest in engineering activities such as designing, building, and analyzing *(spatial skills, creativity)*. However, there is a stark difference in many girls' comfort with tools and technology (including computers and machinery) and their interest in applying their knowledge to areas that don't directly benefit humans.[8] Thus, if you want to encourage your girl into engineering, provide more opportunities to play with and practice with the tools and technology to help her become more confident. This is especially effective if she works with others on meaningful projects. Together, these experiences can foster a strong desire to endure the educational hardships. The ability to help others is largely the reason that women cite for enduring the difficulties of medical school. When I was a girl, only about 25% of medical students were women, but today, their representation is nearly equal that of men's.

Also, a positive social experience is key for girls to "stick through" the inevitable difficult hurdles. This can be done through clubs, school, or social groups with supportive, engaged and similarly interested friends (often girlfriends).[9] This may need to be maintained through college, graduate school, and the workplace.

If you have a boy:

Boys are 30% less likely than girls to complete school[10] and are not pursuing higher education at comparable rates. They usually can work in high-paying physical labor jobs such as construction and manufacturing, but as these jobs decline, education will become more important.[11]

This spells trouble for boys, who in general have more troubles staying still and focused; boys are 4-5 times more likely than girls to be diagnosed with ADHD. The hands-on, get-it-working, try-and-try-again nature of engineering leverages boys' tendencies to make, break, and move around. Engineering in school can motivate boys' interest in science, math, and team communication. Since they use end goals to set an "internal compass," aiming for an engineering career can help them surmount hurdles.[9]

Things you can do

Provide opportunities to experience everyday tools and technology:

- materials (wood, plastic, clay)
- electronic or mechanical equipment (cameras, computers, breadboards, multimeters, microprocessors.)
- power supplies (candles, lemon, salt water, or alkaline batteries)
- manufacturing tools (scissors, hammers, saws, glue guns, staplers, soldering irons)

If you have a girl:

- Be a learning companion or encourage her to do projects with friends that have them dream big, overcome obstacles, and manage risk.
- Share stories of women who engineered things, including fictional ones like Violet in Lemony Snickett's tales.

If you have a boy:

- Help him find a purpose for his learning, such as engineering careers or projects.
- Connect schoolwork with his goals; help him develop coping skills.

Limited Economic Resources

From my experience with both urban and rural parents and teachers, I know that getting the resources and experiences for kids with limited finances is a challenge. But the effort is worthwhile. In fact, the United States has always looked to the initiative and drive of all its people, no matter their initial economic standing. Engineers can come from financially strapped families, as evidenced by civil engineer Thomas Telford, mechanical engineer Karl Benz, and agricultural engineer George Washington Carver.

Education historically has been seen as a way to break out of economically challenged situations,[12] but it requires coordinated efforts by families, teachers, and communities. Furthermore, money for living is only one difficulty financially strapped kids encounter on the road to engineering. Community schools they attend are usually under-resourced and have inadequate curricula to make students "engineering eligible." Social situations may be complicated by related crime, drugs, and gangs.[13]

Financially disadvantaged students can gain relevant experiences in elementary and secondary school in after-school and summer camps through schools, museums, or neighboring colleges. Many of these programs offer scholarships for children in need. Science competitions or invention fairs can help kids meet and learn from other interested engineers and students and gain exposure to expert feedback. These are good experiences to put on college applications, as they show a level of involvement beyond the classroom.

Students from financially strapped backgrounds are often the first in their family to go to college. It is important to find teachers, guidance counselors, and older students to mentor them through financial aid, college expectations, utilizing the available academic support and resources, and balancing family, work and school.

These students are truly breaking new ground and need to be able to take full advantage of all the opportunities available to them.

A few key guidelines while navigating the resources:

- *Exposure:* Find opportunities for your kid to explore engineering through after-school activities, summer camps, and day-long programs. They can serve the dual purpose of letting your kid experience engineering as well as getting him or her to see and interact with practicing engineers who may have information on future opportunities. Encourage your kid to enter competitions or fairs, regardless if he or she wins. Well-known ones like LEGO League, FIRST Robotics, Destination Imagination, Odyssey of the Mind, Future City, Siemens Westinghouse Science and Technology, or Intel Science Talent Search have clear guidelines that help kids develop more sophisticated approaches to pursuing and presenting engineering problems. These can open more opportunities locally. Hackathons and outreach events by professional organizations, universities, and companies are also good ways to expose kids to engineering experiences.

- *Community:* Create a supportive community for your kid and his or her friends through parent groups, teacher-parent organizations, or community groups. Together, you can find academic resources for your child.

- *Mentoring:* Through your community, set up mentoring venues with teachers, guidance counselors, other parents, or older students who have gone to college. Connect them with your child so they can advise him or her on the mental, physical, financial, and spiritual challenges that may be encountered while preparing for college or engineering.

- *Financial Advising:* Work with community groups and mentors to identify ways you can get more resources for your school or for college. Consider whether the military might be an option. Explicitly recommend students for scholarships or special programs that will give them exposure and experience.

Racial Stereotypes

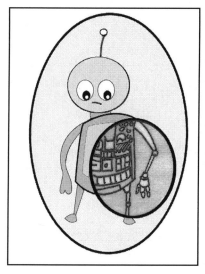

Even though I am a racial minority (Asian American, or Chinese, to be exact) my experience is vastly different from my African American, Hispanic American, and Native American colleagues.

These groups are growing in the country's overall population but are very small in engineering professions. This is why they are referred to as "underrepresented."

The situation for many kids from these three groups is complicated by low economic status, which affects their access to engineering. These kids often have not taken required math and science courses needed to start engineering college programs, either because of their ability to complete the courses in high school or because the school has not provided those opportunities. Studies indicate that only 4% of African American, Hispanic American, and Native American children were "engineering eligible."[14]

Although all humans are the same inside—there is no "race" gene—some kids face difficulties simply because of their race: prejudices about the intellectual capacity of certain racial groups exist even at school. This can be dangerous, since teachers and counselors play as important a role as families for encouraging kids into engineering. The effect is pronounced for kids whose parents are not college-educated and can only encourage them in a general direction towards college.[15]

Interestingly, the representation of non-white women in engineering is higher than that for the white population.[14] Figuring out how to entice and prepare women in minority populations sheds light on how to encourage all children into engineering, regardless of gender, race, or ethnicity. With the inevitable increase in non-white persons in the American workforce, removing barriers to engineering for makes good economic sense.[16]

Things you can do

- *Parents:* Encourage and support your kid to take the math and science necessary to become engineering eligible. Be a role model by taking on your own educational and personal challenges.

- *Teachers:* Talk explicitly about engineering as a possible major and career. Talk about engineering in terms of helping community or providing financial stability for family. Reflect on how to identify and address unconscious prejudices or restricting actions. Help kids learn to find and create supportive social environments in new situations. Find role models or their stories from engineering societies (NSBE, AISES, SHPE, SASE). Work with kids and families on specific solutions to areas needing improvement rather than presenting abstract suggestions.

Language and Culture Issues

My parents were new immigrants who decided to speak only English to me. As a result, I sadly cannot speak Cantonese so have first-hand experience of what it is like not to understand the language being used. I felt stupid (even though I wasn't) and frustrated because few of my family members thought to stop and translate discussions or decisions that were said in Chinese.

For many Hispanic, Asian, and new immigrant families, language and culture create educational issues. Some speak a different language at home, so they are considered behind in English-language literacy. Sometimes the cultural norms of the kids treat teachers, schools, and supervisors as authority figures who can be trusted to treat them fairly; this backfires if teachers have unconscious prejudices.[17] Culture can also discourage kids from engineering if gender expectations are restrictive. College application and attendance become more difficult for those who believe that talking about achievements is impolite or that it is wrong to ask for or receive financial aid.

My mother, in her wisdom, made me give presentations to and share candy with my classmates every Chinese New Year. From doing so I figured out how my perspectives and values were shaped, which helped me balance my Chinese culture with the American world in which I lived. These experiences helped me practice talking about cultural differences with my peers so we could find ways to respect and understand each other.

Strong cultural identities can motivate kids into engineering if they see engineering as a way to help their community or provide for their families. Having a wider representation of different cultures and values in engineering is also important for innovation. Some have argued that if more Native Americans were engineers, we could have developed eco-friendly products and systems earlier because of the value that their cultures often place on the earth.

Things you can do

- *Parents:* Encourage kids to share their language and culture as well as learn about others'. Work on your own English language skills and help teachers learn useful phrases in your language.

- *Teachers:* Avoid making negative or positive assumptions about kids from different cultures. Try to learn kids' languages. This may help you communicate with parents, and will also let kids know that their language is worth knowing. For kids with low confidence, putting them in the teacher's seat may help them feel that they know something and may give them insight into how hard it is to teach someone else. Bring in professional engineers who share similar language, culture, or experiences as your kids. Pause to consider what cultural assumptions you may be making.

Physical Limitations

Physical disabilities range from mobility impairments (e.g., paralysis, missing limbs) to sensory impairments (e.g., deafness, blindness). Everyday life activities need to be done differently, and access to education can become difficult: reading books, attending lecture, or moving around in lab can be a real challenge for those who cannot see, hear, or move easily. Worrying about how to get to places on the school campus can distract a disabled person from his or her studies: imagine propelling a wheelchair through a snow-filled walkway or not being able to reach the top of a lab bench.

Additionally, when these kids enter school or the workforce, misconceptions can prevent a productive environment. Teachers may delay the process of teaching math in favor of communication skills (e.g., sign language or Braille). While seemingly reasonable in one sense, delaying the basics extends the timeline for more complex and abstract concepts, resulting in low math achievement even at basic levels.[18] This is then compounded by negative preconceptions about students' abilities, when the real problem is the lack of new techniques appropriate for different methods of communication.[19]

Why bother encouraging those with physical disabilities? For one thing, they often have highly developed engineering traits: *perseverance* and *creative problem solving* are familiar because they are used every single day. They often also have the wisdom to *communicate* when help is needed while maintaining a healthy dose of self-determination. I have found that students who have taken on their physical challenges carry that determination to their coursework. Self-awareness, self-confidence, and handling stress are all side benefits, so to speak, of having a disability.

Persons with disabilities have brought valuable perspectives to general product development. Today we all reap the benefit of these technologies: voice recognition software, scanning systems that read text out loud, closed captioning, stairclimbing machines, Segway personal transporters, ramps, automatic door openers, and computers controlled by eye movement. A person with physical limitations can be both user and engineer for the next new innovative product.

Things you can do

- Ensure your kid is keeping up on math and science lessons. For the mobility-impaired kid, this may mean making sure that lab or computer equipment is accessible, especially if group work is the norm. It is important for kids to be able to take equal responsibility in the work.

- For the sensory-impaired kid, this may mean making sure teachers spend as much time with the math and science lessons. It is important for the deaf interpreter to understand the material, not just translate the words. Recognize that mathematics is sometimes difficult because words have different, precise meanings in mathematics. For example, "square" and "root" have different meanings in everyday life than in mathematics. "If and only if" is a very precise situation and cannot be substituted with "if."[18] When possible, make the mathematics tangible. Put real objects in the kid's hands to build a connection between abstract concepts of numbers and shapes with the physical reality.

- If problems arise in learning, work as a team (kid, teachers, parents) to figure out viable solutions. This is a great opportunity to put engineering to work for you, because sometimes the solution is a technical one or a system that can be defined to foster success. Check out the latest adaptive or assistive technologies available on the web (e.g., www.pacer.org or www.assistivetechnologies.com).

- Encourage your kid to talk about frustrations or problems encountered, guiding him or her to possible solutions (as in my story in Chapter 2). Use the Engineering Design Process to try out different ideas, and don't get discouraged if a solution is not found on the first try. Empower your kid to create solutions to the problems that stand in his or her way today.

- Find and share success stories of how problems faced by those with physical limitations were solved. This includes fiction (I grew up on *The Great Brain* by John D. Fitzgerald), non-fiction (my mother bought me *Wren* by Marie Killilea and *Don't Feel Sorry for Paul* by Bernard Wolf), and web pages (search for "stories on disabled in engineering").

Pulling It All Together

Though most of the traits required of engineering are natural for most kids, there are a lot of reasons people believe engineering isn't for everyone. Certainly, not everyone will be interested or passionate about it. However, if your kid gets the engineering itch, it's important to make sure the door isn't closed to your kid because of biological, social, economic, or cultural reasons. Imagine where we would be if Thomas Edison believed he really was addle-brained and useless or if Lillian Gilbreth accepted her father's limited plans for herself.

While these conditions may create some challenges for your kid, they shouldn't be barriers. Meeting these challenges will give your kid a unique perspective that will be a valuable asset in the world of engineering. As Edison said: "Many of life's failures are people who did not realize how close they were to success when they gave up."

It is important to remember that we live our lives as whole people, not as categories. Even as you focus on the characteristics that make your kid a unique individual, remember how complex identities are. Not all girls or all boys face the same issues: a boy from a family with limited economic resources faces challenges that a middle-class boy does not. An immigrant girl faces different challenges from those of a girl born in the U.S. As you think about the statistics and other information presented in this chapter, keep in mind the interconnections within your kid as you work with him or her in thinking about engineering.

Things you can do

Stay focused on the *real* barriers that keep all kids from seeing engineering as an option:

- Access to quality education

- Experiences that lead to innovative approaches to meaningful problems

- Practice working with a wide range of people with different backgrounds and approaches

This is an exciting time. The sense of national urgency for engineering will present another opportunity to break through unconscious assumptions and prejudices. This won't be the first time an attitude adjustment has helped increase technical experiences and opportunities for everyone. In World War II, women and racial minority groups were given educational and training opportunities (Rosie the Riveter; Tuskegee Airmen). It is important for us to seize every opportunity to help those previously denied access to engineering-related education.

If you have built castles in the air, your work need not be lost; that is where they should be. Now put foundations under them.
—Henry David Thoreau

Whether your kids are already on the path towards engineering or they need a little encouragement, there are a few things you can do to support them at home and at school. It's never too early to start, and your kids will benefit from your support throughout their journey. The nature of this support changes as kids age, but in a way, it is no different from the kind that's given for sports. The touchstones are the same:

Exposure: Every Olympic athlete I learn about started with the sport early. Likewise, continual exposure to engineering in the everyday world will help your kid see the marvelous ways in which engineering relates to life. Encourage your kid with your own curiosity and excitement by asking questions that will stimulate the imagination.

Relevance: In Chinese martial-arts movies, the skills learned in training are used to make other life tasks easier: for example, the young monk realizes that chores become infinitely easier if he applies all the skills and perspectives he developed through practice. When you show that learning engineering makes school easier (and even interesting), the engineering spark will come to life. View the question "So what?" or "What is it good for?" as the sign of a blossoming engineer.

Foundation and Practice: All sports require basic skills such as catching, throwing, hitting, and running. Engineering is the same. Keep kids focused on making progress, at whatever pace is right for them. Remind them that smart kids know practice is important—just ask Michael Jordan! Talent is useless if it's not perfected and used. Don't let them quit if they don't achieve perfection on the first try.

Let's look at some other ways you can support your kids as they start their engineering journey.

At Home

- **Be a learning companion** (*"Let's figure it out together"*)[1]:
  I can't tell you how many engineering friends have stories of working on projects with their parents or family members. I handed tools to my father, cooked with my mother, and worked on electronics projects with my sister, showing her how to solder and read assembly instructions. *Other projects:* putting up shelves, balancing a checkbook, planning a holiday party, or researching which car, dishwasher, or toolkit to buy. *Tips:* When problem solving, talk out loud so your kid hears your thought process. Write or draw ideas on paper so that they see what you "see" in your head. Each of these activities provides experience with building and fixing things, working with others, communicating technical information, and building confidence in getting things done.

- **Take your kid on outings, to camps, or to classes:** Go to the park, the zoo, museums, lakes/ocean, rivers, and air shows. This exposes your kid to how engineering is used in life and provides experiences that teachers can refer to in science and math class to give the concepts context. Have your kid help you read the map to get there and get around. Keep a Question Notebook in a bag/backpack or the car where your kid can write questions that arise while on the outing. Find an engineering (or science or math) camp or class that has a comfortable social setting for your kid. It's important that he or she socializes with others while doing engineering. This helps kids realize what they can accomplish with others, associates engineering with positive social experiences, and helps them find "their people." -

- **Play games, do kits, and build models:** The best way to practice is through play. Games that enhance memory skills, visio-spatial abilities, math abilities, strategy, problem solving and construction skills are great ways to help kids to solidify the basic traits that keep the engineering door open. See the Resources section for some of my favorite staple activities.

- **Keep a "take-apart box" or "touch box":** If you are a pack rat like me, nothing could be easier. I keep a box of old broken items (plastic cases, an old mixer, a burnt out drill, dried out pens) for students to take apart. That way you don't have to worry about them breaking anything. While they take it apart, they are able to learn how things work. The touch box is for kids with "itchy fingers"—they can't keep their hands off things. This instinct is a good one, but sometimes it's not appropriate for them to touch everything they encounter. The touch box can be their treasure trove of things that are okay for them to touch, pull, squish, etc. This stimulates curiosity and helps them figure out the material properties of objects, which they can use in their future engineering projects.

At School

- Be an advocate for your kid by partnering with the teachers, and work to help your kid meet educational standards. For better or worse, standards are used to determine "engineering eligibility."

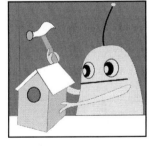

- Look for after-school activities that will help your kid learn and develop the engineering traits. This can include sports and crafts, not just robotics.

- Work with your child to establish a good foundation in the skills that will be required in school topics later (math, science, communication, hand-eye coordination, visio-spatial skills).

In Elementary School (Preschool–5th grade)

- ***Encourage an iterative process:*** If a kid can graduate from 3rd grade realizing that good work requires iteration (multiple tries), that kid will do well. Too many kids seem to think that the smart students do their assignments right the first time. Help them get the idea that any kind of iteration (e.g., drafts or prototypes) is actually a good thing.

- ***Encourage the use of basic technology and tools:*** Experience with technologies such as material (paper, clay, metal), power (batteries, hand cranks), instruments (microscope, telescope, stethoscope, magnifying glass) and computers (Scripts in Word, formulas in spreadsheets, HTML in blog posts), develops engineering instincts. These are the "tool kits" kids can use to solve problems in the future. Use of tools such as scissors, glue, tape, hammers, saws, drills, and nails complements other building skills such as tearing, folding, and drawing. Some kids use their technology (a glue gun, a magnifying glass, or a rubber boat) so much that they get attached to it and carry it around everywhere. I have even known some kids to sleep with these objects! As odd as this may seem, attachment to objects is one of the best ways to establish internal motivation that persists into future endeavors.[2] This continues throughout life, as I have seen college students develop confidence and excitement about their abilities in engineering when they attach to their tools and devices.

In Middle School (6th grade–8th grade)

Point out to kids how education helps them engineer their projects more efficiently. Not only will higher levels of science and math help them, but their more sophisticated language skills will help them brainstorm, research, and document better. They should see that learning from and defriefing with others helps save time compared to the random trial-and-error method they may have used alone. Show them how documenting their own work is a way for others to see their vision and help them in the future.

In High School (9th grade–12th grade)

Make sure kids get into the required courses in math (at least trigonometry, possibly some calculus), science (at least one year each of chemistry and physics), computers (at least an introduction to scripting like HTML or programming such as JavaScript), and industrial arts (technical drawing, machining, or woodshop would help). This helps them become eligible for college engineering programs.

In College

Besides determining what location and institution size they would like, help kids find the right mix of teaching styles for their best learning:

- **University** ("Sage on the Stage"): The traditional "lecture" style is effective for transferring information to a large audience. For some, this style is ideal. For engineers, this includes lecture, labs, homework assignments, and tests with occasional projects. This style often generates the idea of seeking "answers" to posed questions.

- **Socratic/Confucian** ("Guide on the Side"): This is an older form of teaching that places more of the learning and questioning responsibility on the student. Today, this is sometimes referred to as inquiry-based learning. Students develop their own questions and use professors and teaching assistants as coaches (in the early stages) and consultants (in the latter stages). This style often fosters the idea of learning coming from within the individual. Students in this system need to feel comfortable with the non-linear process of discovery and invention.

- ***Apprentice/Project-based*** ("Learn by Doing and Watching"): This is also an older form of teaching, derived from the craft guilds. It includes demonstration of how to do common practices, how to approach common problems through recitations or practice problem sessions, and how to operate in the lab, as well as time to practice skills. Together, they develop skills required for the larger senior project.

Depending on the institution, students may be expected to enter with a certain level of experience with tools and technologies. Some institutions will tie engineering projects closely with business, either through a business school or actual companies. Often, colleges have a different mix of each of these styles.

No matter where your kid goes, make sure he or she will use familiar learning styles as well as develop less familiar ones. Helping kids have a wide range of learning strategies under their belts is the best way you can help them on the road to success.

Parting Thoughts

Whew! That's a lot of information. I felt this book was needed because so many people I meet confess that they don't really know what engineering is. Knowing about engineering is an important first step in encouraging any kid in engineering. It helps you become a built-in support system for your kid. I hope that this blend of stories, research, and suggestions has answered some of the questions you have about engineering, especially as it relates to your own kid.

This book was a labor of love for me, mainly because engineering is an important part of my life. It has shaped the way I think about things and how I approach the world. However, as a former professor and now an IT analyst, I obviously am not a practicing engineer anymore. Apparently, I'm not the only one. When I went back for college reunions, only one of my five engineering lab partners was still doing something technical. One was a VP for a game distributor, another a manager in the biomedical industry, a third a director at the FBI, and the last a post-modernist dancer. Who knows—at a future reunion, one might head up a large company like Xerox's or DuPont's current CEOs, or be President of the United States, like Herbert Hoover or Jimmy Carter!

The lesson is clear: Engineering is only one step in a life journey. Majoring in it does not lock your kid into one narrow career; in fact, it opens up many other options. And that's what education is all about, in general—opening up possibilities.

Congratulations! You can now consider yourself initiated into the world of engineering— hopefully you will never look at the world around you in the same way again. I hope you enjoy the rest of your journey!

For me, engineering started with stories. In particular, I remember how these books influenced me in my youth. I can't tell you how many times these fiction classics helped me put context to my engineering education.

Toddler to Pre-School

- *Paddle to the Sea.* I still remember the technical drawings about the lock and dam and the lumber mill. I was a mechanical geek even back then.
- *Mike Mulligan and His Steam Shovel.* I distinctly remember the annotated diagrams in the end papers of the hardback book showing the different controls of Mary Anne, the steam shovel.
- *Katy and the Big Snow.* Bulldozer characteristics as well as map concepts pepper the illustrations.
- *Bears in the Night* and *Inside, Outside, Upside Down.* Talk about spatial words! Practice gesturing while you read these classics.

Elementary School

- *Island of the Blue Dolphins.* What if you were stranded on island by yourself? Talk about the need for engineering. And it's a girl!
- *Little House in the Big Woods* and the other books. I learned how people lived and made things before there was electricity, automobiles, or any kind of infrastructure like running water. I recently used *The Long Winter* to illustrate several examples of the engineering design process in a curriculum I developed.
- *The Great Brain* books. Though Tom used his great brain to con kids, he does use his understanding of how the world works towards a goal. And I got to learn how toilets worked, how ice cream was made, and how to use the engineering design process to help a disabled friend.
- *The Boxcar Children.* I actually only liked the first book because that was when the kids had nothing. I learned how they made their own home, wagon, and refrigerator.
- *Encyclopedia Brown* books. I was so addicted to these. Encyclopedia used his understanding of how the world works, strong observation skills, and logical prowess to solve mysteries for kids.

Throughout childhood, encourage your child to be a participant in the engineering-trait-rich activities you do, even if it is as a spectator or "helper." Remember, engineering traits are used in even mundane activities like changing batteries in devices (*spatial reasoning, tools and technology*), programming the clock or DVR (*math, science, tools and technology, creativity, communication*), creating Halloween decorations (*math, perseverance, problem solving tools and technology, spatial skills creativity*), or building the shelves or furniture kits you get at the store (*math, science, spatial reasoning, communication, perseverance, problem solving, tools and technology*).

Keeping Engineering Interest Alive

Once the interest is stimulated, there are a lot of great resources to keep the interest going and to develop the traits. For an ever-updated list of books and other resources, visit the Engineer's Playground Pinterest page at www.pinterest.com/engineersplay

The site is organized to provide resources for different stages of engineering development. The "Start Seeing STEM" board contains history, movie, literature, and art connections to engineering and are great starting places for kids to recognize and develop the engineering process. Some are best for young ages, but others can be appropriate for late-comers—older kids who are new to engineering. Many can also be great "novelty" gifts for your older, well-rounded engineer.

Developing those 8 traits needed by engineers can be done while doing things that may not look like engineering. These boards focus on some of the standard ways you can generate interest, develop foundational understanding, and maybe even geek out through games, toys, kits, and simulations:

- Easy to Access STEM
- Math/Visual Spatial STEM Resources
- Physics/Electromechanical STEM Resources
- STEM Resources for Learning About Computers

Once your kid is hooked, you will need resources and opportunities to develop the talent:
- STEM Supplies/Project Resources
- STEM Competitions/Organizations/Scholarships

Chapter 1: What Is This Thing Called Engineering?

1. Schwarz, F. D. (2000). Art, craft, and engineering. *American Heritage of Invention and Technology, 16*(1). Retrieved from http://www.inventionandtech.com/content/arts-and-crafts-and-engineering-1

2. Gilbert, C. G. & Eyring, M. J. (2010, May). Beating the odds when you launch a new venture. *Harvard Business Review*, 93-98. Retrieved from https://hbr.org/2010/05/beating-the-odds-when-you-launch-a-new-venture

Chapter 2: How Do Kids Prepare for Engineering?

1. ABET, Inc. (2016). *Criteria for accrediting applied science programs.* Retrieved from http://www.abet.org/accreditation/accreditation-criteria/criteria-for-accrediting-engineering-programs-2016-2017/

2. Schreuders, P. D., Mannon, S. E. & Rutherford, B. (2009). Pipeline or personal preference: women in engineering. *European Journal of Engineering Education, 34*(1), 97-112.

3. Turkle, S. (2008, May 20). A passion for objects. *The Chronicle of Higher Education, 54*(38), B11.

4. Lahart, J. (2009, Nov 13). Tinkering makes comeback amid crisis. *Wall Street Journal.* Retrieved from https://www.wsj.com/articles/SB125798004542744219

5. Root-Bernstein, M. & Root-Bernstein, R. (2009, Oct 29). Can women be creative scientists? The danger of testing for creative ability. [Blog] Retrieved from https://www.psychologytoday.com/blog/imagine/200910/can-women-be-creative-scientists-the-dangers-testing-creative-ability

6. Park, G., Lubinski, D., & Benbow, C. P. (2010, Nov 2). Recognizing spatial intelligence. *Scientific American.* Retrieved from https://www.scientificamerican.com/article/recognizing-spatial-intel/

7. Root-Bernstein, R., Allen, L., Beach, L. Badhula, R., Fast, J., Hosey, C. ... Weinlander, S. (2008). Arts foster scientific success: Avocations of Nobel, National Academy, Royal Society, and Sigma Xi members. *Psychology Today.* Retrieved from https://www.google.com/url?sa=t&rct=j&q=&esrc=s&source=web&cd=1&cad=rja&uact=8&ved=0ahUKEwjyutuDrr_VAhVq2oMKHRfSCeQQFggrMAA&url=https%3A%2F%2Fwww.psychologytoday.com%2Ffiles%2Fattachments%2F1035%2Farts-foster-scientific-success.pdf&usg=AFQjCNF_UvzLIxV2xC2dNGIjxxUykvkSrQ

Chapter 3: What Would My Kid Do as an Engineer?

1. Engineers Dedicated to a Better Tomorrow. (2007, Feb). *A brief guide to engineering majors.* Retrieved from http://www.dedicatedengineers.org/Resources/Engineering_Disciplines_Handout.pdf

Chapter 4: Who Says My Kid Can't Do Engineering?

1. Tobias, S. (1993). *Overcoming math anxiety:* revised and expanded. New York, NY: W.W. Norton & Company.

2. Sorby, S. (2001). A course in spatial visualization and its impact on the retention of female engineering students. *Journal of Women and Minorities in Science and Engineering, 7,* 153-172.

3. Paul, A. M. (2012, Jun 22). *How thinking in 3D can improve math and science skills.* Retrieved from https://ww2.kqed.org/mindshift/2012/06/22/how-spatial-thinking-can-improve-math-and-science-skills/

4. Smith, M., Robinson, L., & Segal, J. (2017). *ADHD in children.* Retrieved on Aug 5, 2017 from https://www.helpguide.org/articles/add-adhd/attention-deficit-disorder-adhd-in-children.htm?pdf=true

5. Kemp, G., Smith, M., & Segal, J. (2017). *Learning disabilities and disorders.* Retrieved on Aug 5, 2017 from https://www.helpguide.org/articles/autism-learning-disabilities/learning-disabilities-and-disorders.htm?pdf=true

6. Loftus, M. (2010, Summer). In their grasp. *Prism.* Retrieved from http://www.prism-magazine.org/summer10/feature_02.cfm

7. Hendricks, M. (2005, Sep 1). Disorderly conduct. *Entrepreneur.* Retrieved from https://www.entrepreneur.com/article/79342

8. Schreuders, P. D., Mannon, S. E., & Rutherford B. (2009, Mar). Pipeline or personal preference: women in engineering. *European Journal of Engineering Education. 34*(1), 97-112.

9. Lee, J. D. (2002, Oct). More than ability: Gender and personal relationships influence science and technology involvement. *Sociology of Education, 75*(4), 349-373.

10. PBS Parents. (2003-2017). *Understanding and raising boys: Boys in school.* Retrieved from http://www.pbs.org/parents/raisingboys/school.html

11. Schepp, D. (2010, Jan 25). *People@work: The great recession is worse for men.* Retrieved from https://www.aol.com/2010/01/25/people-work-the-great-recession-is-worse-for-men/

12. Maier, P., Smith, M. R., Keyssar, A., & Kevles, D. (2006). *Inventing America: A history of the United States (Vol. 1),* 2nd ed. New York: NY: W.W. Norton & Company, Inc.

13. Pellino, K. M. (2007). *The effects of poverty on teaching and learning*. Retrieved from http://www.teach-nology.com/tutorials/teaching/poverty/

14. Frehill, L. M., DiFabio, N. M., & Hill, S. T. (2008, May). *Confronting the "new" American dilemma: Underrepresented minorities in engineering: A data-based look at diversity*. White Plains, NY: National Action Council for Minorities in Engineering, Inc. (NACME).

15. Trenor, J. M. and Yu, S. L. (2008). Diversity within diversity. *Prism, 51*. Retrieved from http://www.prism-magazine.org/dec08/tt_02.cfm

16. Wilson, V. (2016, Jun 9). *People of color will be a majority of the American working class in 2032*. Retrieved from http://www.epi.org/publication/the-changing-demographics-of-americas-working-class/

17. Gasbarra, P. & Johnson, J. (2008). *Out before the game begins: Hispanic leaders talk about what's needed to bring more Hispanic youngsters into science, technology and math professions*. Palisades, NY: Public Agenda. Retrieved from ERIC Database. (ED501564)

18. Kelly, R. R. & Faustad, M. G. (2006, Aug 10). Deaf college student' mathematical skills relative to morphological knowledge, reading level and language proficiency. *Journal of Deaf Studies and Deaf Education, 12*(1), 25-37. doi:10.1093/deafed/enl012 or https://www.ncbi.nlm.nih.gov/pubmed/16901954

19. Beal, C. R. & Shaw, E. (2008, Mar). Working memory and math problem solving by blind middle and high school students: Implications for universal access. *Proceedings of the 19th International Conference of the Society for Information Technology and Teacher Education*. Retrieved from http://citeseerx.ist.psu.edu/viewdoc/download?doi=10.1.1.141.34 10&rep=rep1&type=pdf

Chapter 5: Looking Ahead

1. Damour, L. (2009, Nov 9). Teaching girls to tinker. *Education Week, 29*(11), 25. Retrieved from http://www.edweek.org/ew/articles/2009/11/11/11damour.h29.html

2. Turkle, S. (2008, May 20). A passion for objects. *The Chronicle of Higher Education, 54*(38), B11.

Acknowledgements

This book is the result of the effort and experience of so many people in my life. These include:

My wonderful editor, Luna Shyr, who hit me with her best shot. Thanks so much for taking the manuscript while you were abroad and giving it a good working over with your red pen. You truly are a masterful wordsmith and a great friend.

My patient illustrators, Jack Sutter and Mary Lofgren, who made the words come to life with vibrant and whimsical images. Thanks so much for working with my not-so-clear ideas and constant textual changes. Your perspective and contribution has been invaluable to this project.

My many teachers, in and out of engineering, whether you were my favorite or my less than favorite. As Confucius said, both the person you want to be and the person you don't want to be are important to becoming the person you are.

My dear friends, engineering and otherwise. Thanks to my non-engineering friends, students, and colleagues, especially those at St. Kate's, who gave me such good perspective when I could not see past my engineering blinders. You kept me grounded and relevant. Thanks to my engineering friends for sharing with me the joy, passion, and frustrations you had with engineering. You helped widen my perspective and approach to the field. In particular, thank you, Jennifer Rexford, for being willing to philosophize, metacognize (is that a word?), and analyze about engineering in ways that others would find strange. It was natural to do it with you, and I enjoyed the hours we wasted on it!

My most favorite sister, Celeste, who encouraged me to keep writing, even when life seemed so hopeless. Thanks also for letting me experiment on you and for giving me great perspective on what I really was trying to say about engineering.

My loving parents, Lily and Daniel. Mom, you showed me how fascinating the world is and how I can take an active part in it. I know that you would have made a great engineer, if only your university accepted women in the engineering program, but I think you turned out just great! Dad, even though you are gone, you are far from forgotten. I know that you didn't feel any of your children followed in your science footsteps, but I will always appreciate the support you gave, despite the fact that I stubbornly decided to go my own way.

And finally my husband, Troy. Thank you for pushing me to write it all down, pointing out "that needs to go into your book" and patiently waiting to read the text in its more final form. I am lucky to have such an "appropriate" husband and I'm glad I broke my rule about dating engineers for you.

Yvonne Ng is an engineering education consultant, toy designer, and author who combines practical insights with creative approaches to developing STEM skills in children of all ages. After more than a decade as a mechanical engineer, Ng shifted her focus to education in 2000, joining St. Catherine University, a women's college in St. Paul, Minnesota, as an assistant professor of computer science and engineering. She served as Executive Director of the school's National Center for STEM Elementary Education in 2012.

Ng played a key role in St. Catherine's groundbreaking Science, Technology, Engineering and Mathematics (STEM) initiatives. She helped develop the university's interdisciplinary STEM curriculum, which includes graduate certificates in STEM for both traditional and Montessori teachers — the first program of its kind in the nation.

Ng appeared in the PBS Emmy-nominated series *SciGirls* and co-edited *She's an Engineer? Princeton Alumnae Reflect*, in which female engineers share their stories of working in the field. She recently developed toys (Start Up Circuits for toddlers and Code Hopper for preschoolers) and has two forthcoming children's books (*The Mighty Steam Engine* and *They're Tearing Up Mulberry Street*). She holds a bachelor's degree in mechanical and aerospace engineering from Princeton University and a master's in mechanical engineering from the University of Minnesota.

In 2011, Ng founded Engineer's Playground LLC to help make engineering accessible to a wider audience. Through the Engineer's Playground Website (www.engineersplayground.com), books, toys, and consultations, Ng offers advice, activities and lesson ideas to nurture and develop the lively curiosity and hands-on abilities that make children natural engineers.

Her goal is to help inspire future generations of engineers and scientists, particularly at a time when STEM skills are in high demand.

Made in the USA
Columbia, SC
25 September 2022

67926907R00037